for Basil + Robyn

genrecide

KILLS
POETRY
DEAD

w/ all my love
+ textasis blessings
+ gratitude

adeena karasick

talonbooks

1996

Copyright © 1996 Adeena Karasick

Published with the assistance of the Canada Council.

Talonbooks
#104—3100 Production Way
Burnaby, British Columbia
Canada V5A 4R4

Printed and bound in Canada by Hignell Printing Ltd.

First Printing: October 1996

Canadian Cataloguing in Publication Data
Karasick, Adeena, 1965-
   Genrecide

   Poems.
   ISBN 0-88922-370-X

   I. Title.
PS8571.A74G46 1996   C811'.54   C96-910506-1
PR9199.3.K36546 1996

Previous editions of these texts have appeared in *Prairie Fire, Index, Revival: Spoken Word Anthology from Lollapalooza 94, Agency, Filling Station, Corridors: the Concordia Anthology, The Link, DaDaBaby, Front Lines Anthology of Action Poetry, Carnival: Scream in High Park Reader, Tessera (Dispositions), Chain (Hybrid Genre Issue), Torque*. Portions of *Genrecide* have also appeared as "Of Poetik Thinking" (conference proceedings from the *Applied Derrida Conference*, Luton, UK, 1996); as "Genesis After Babel" (from the *International Symposium on Electronic Art*, Montreal, 1995) and as a CD ROM Virtuality Project (*URGO: A Bonfire*, produced by Chris Bell).

Thanks also to the United Nations Development Program: Malawi, The Banff Center for Performing Arts, Concordia University, Toronto Arts Council, Ontario Arts Council, Canada Council, BC Book Awards, the Malawi Literary Festival and to *Writing the Self Out of Silence* (York University). To Anna Gelbert, Lee Gotham, Blaine Speigel, Christopher Cauley, Jill Battson, Tomeq Michalak, bill bissett and Jonas Chilolo of the Lilongwe villa, Ken Karasick, RMJ Josephson, Evan Karasick, Pine Sol™, Canada Post. To Sharon Nelson for indispensible help with proofreading. And to Karl and Christy at Talon for ongoing support and careful execution of this text.

And special thanks to Sean Southey for yr incredible patience generosity and dedication to this project.

for warren
in memorium

and to *"the intolerable, loved, already known*
which cannot be quoted only incorporated"

(Jacques Derrida)

and to all the letters, their shapes, combined and separated,
swaddled letters, curved ones and crooked ones, superfluous
and elliptic ones, minute and large ones, and inverted. To the
calligraphy of the letters, the open and the closed pericopes, to
the absences, scissions, ciphers and vacancies.

Floruit Retinue

Breached in the folds of

        coptic qua.
   heft sediment wrenched in

a récit precis
of fabricated proclivity licks
or a condiment ditty slit

        her wet secreta wall-newt water
        sallets, swallow specters
        scourged by a sequent axiom
        eked out of fen-sucked fogs slop-foppery

And she was grinding her constitutive contaminants
in a nuance errance

a contrapuntal merge urgency
resurgency

and brims with hiatus smut splurged
in the dyssemetry of desire
in the langour of

a lagubrious ruse
or a sluice with a fuse

'cause she got

a sacrificial scission schizm
where flagrant vagrant plague angling hangs

Like a suspended pudenda
whose syllipsis
insinuant, prospicuous.

A recidivist with a twist.

And her syntagm smiles

in iterable determinants, torrents
entropic exigencies 'cause acumen
sagacity or accuracy grasp
calculated

in snack bracket cracks
of grammatical slack.

In the interstices as
spurn squall
slakes,

                 swill pilea slip ripples
signs in staggered absences abrasion and
blows

                    in casque cramp
                             scams serum scud comes
                                    in sucked out surfaces
                                            as *simplement* implements

in lisps and distances
as shiftless slips
swing sequences

And slinks in caviat squirm swill slough

as necessity silences
her absence, a border
trussed in the echo of

insurrection
flexion flummoxed in

flagon agon gone,
as a forago ergo ipso else aeons, come

like an inclusive exclusion
emissed in dissolution, adorned

in an anomian home, homiletic
eidetic, echoed in

what's *elle iterate*, cliterate
stretched in the cinder of
criteria hysteria smears.

Squalor

I

In a sepulcheral semiotic of stoichea logoi imbalance,
she was up to her albeit in
prospicuous syllepsis as
please parses plays or pliés propulses
expressly rejected as aeolea aereoli

II

      Crept into astrakhan crockpot paquet plaques. Picket proxy cracker plot. Usufruct it up **fuckitup** your cumulous. Pummel me to the tinctures. [Just a little bit harder]. In oesophaegal flagrance: in the gullet of fricative static

III

And locate yr history in
liminal immitants mutated in

fidgets widgets
slippages in / sub umbra umbels
pendulous appendages eolopile ampules.
& park yr impetus in etceteras' edge.

As an exploitative ploy supplies
a moratoria topoi: a
midriff with a lift —
So don't flatter your grand slam spam
by ases, sallies
trenches, basilisks, culverin
currents.

Cause, in a fiction of duration,
in[vag(ue)ination

   you deserve a break today

An inexcusable ruse [incongruous].

IV

My hypollages, i sd
as a trope elopes,
as cut throat cramps, katabatic, cataclinal kick-ass ketosis

Chiquita Burana,

as hypotactic contaminants spasm as liminal splits
relapsi lisps. So, show me the way to go homonyma, anonyma
pneumonema

Cause clearly, incomensurate
echolalia ulcers.

A visceral fixture
in effluvial skew

And one day i knew
propinquitous impugnance nuance strains
as dementia distended in irritant determinants.
So, do *Lettriste* and twist []
Grinding in adage smears hypostacy sluice. Hoop scruples or usurer
ruse. / / Threshold me now, in the sweet lineaments of
surfaces resemblance imbalance
scours. Graçias mass, mercy matrices
in a consequence of anxieties nexes axes

So, hey baby, Yo Baby. Yo Yo Yo

in a semiotic of
splenetics
emetics,
paratactic tacit crypts kickbox
capillary pillow proximity ploys
in gossamer rosters.

Tableaux or not tableaux
that is the question
in a complex of sequitur scars.

Because unduly fettered, i'm
aggressively felching now.

      Concommitant in sequence opulence, clinamen claiment
conduit clues. So, don't flitter your frequent forges fewer fleets by
imbroglio lugubriant briggflat brolly

i'm dreaming of a
mandible sparoid, perorated
in the agon of panoply straps.

Amemiolerated in moebious dyssemia
paroxystic consequence
come, lately.

V

So, work it girl. In transmigratory contiguity. Cause you're inarticulate
as a truncated thrust struggles in a synonymous complex
& i'm telling you]
n illimitable polyp solypse slips
a festival vestibule
Get outta town
Cause i don't don't don't don't want
no filial phalo filo floss
skeptically anaphalectic in radical laxity

Do you read me

no frangipane pinstripe patasticized
n systemic salience.

Nosegay, naysay,
Duvet, as it may—

In subsequent syntax ersatz swill screams
subsalicylo sally slough velcro,

Harangue around the caller.

An escutcheon embusque bust bludgeoned by zyzygy grills. (just wanna
have) ossicle sauce. **Conduit. Ingot.** integument overhang angling a
sepsis pep. trespass. Anathematic pneuma spume. In adjacent drainage,
homonyma anonyma mnemonymy. Onomasti musters / her sweet weave
odium.

Circumfission I
(inter.alias)

I

And before the sun, walls,
windows. Before
dead rivets driven in
a dentata of apparitions
in the virus of
trellis suffices,

diurnal linen lineament
ciphers in the fullness like
a metonymic mimic.

in the definition of
difference, appliance,
appearance,

II

A contagion agency
or contingent exigency.

III

between a title
and a preface. Between substitution and
transference, transgression. Between
a topography of

bequest sequesters
as sonic zest / Fury where the cuts swung / where
no glance strongs past.

IV

In Lilongwe. Takin' la langue way. plus de langue, lingers. As her tongue. kiss*. mouth. closed around ellipse slip. tasting the tongue of a tongue, a tome. L'anglais en Lilongwe. No lily-livered sasparilla suckin' swill way. sways as her tongue, teeth, lips part, solypse sip in prolixis licks; a ventriloquist kiss. in the darkness of slick kissery articulate, as accessory synnexes in the nexus collapses into méconnaises kenosis kinesis askance.

Lilongwe, le *langelait*. In the intimacy of borders tongue.lick.taste. As clavicle hollow slack ex-schize kiss caught in the covets risks *la loi* of Luangwa lingers as Lilongwe or Longueille, eh. As slick limits lip clots distance with desire

où est Lilongwe, l'angue way.

V

As linguae grinds
in the magnate of rhetorical invasion.

---

*   **You must remember this.**
       A kiss is just a kiss. (Casablanca)

16

VI

A ravinous graft
or traumatic masque acts
returns / upon itself
in the midday difference
in the horror of desire

(ne pas de horror) or
abhoria or

As the unspeakable gathers
in replication or
re-application
as infraction, betrayal

in anamnesis,
mnemesis

unheimlich ich:

VII

In the sting of
abdicate covets incurs
in splenetic extension

her supplicant cunning
surfaces in yr cumulous
down. In the matrix of resistence
insistence. Her reticent
dissensus resents

> *that maybe*
> *hot and steamy maybe*

VIII

'cause interstitially speaking,
a misspelled swill of
kichotic crops
in the comma of
request. In the
famine laminate
latrine hydrax jacks,

but the river was wide and i swam it,
'cause damn it, i am it, and i love

when you hunker down
in the genre of

slipstream sucking light
come flummery

in the alliance of
night screws, clamps,
stains, questions,
as if i care in the gnawing
in the envy,

in a surplus of
spectrality, sacrality, alterity

syncretic etiquette
acts in the risk of
fixity [sic]
exits in

IX

yr look or locus
acted out in

      the echo of
      articulation
      in the stain of
      resistence splits

And i hear yr hearing

folds or
faint feign
focusses / fixed as

the reminder or
remainder

             in the economy of a foci loci
               skewhiff riff, as if
               stiffed, an ambient
               pamby sifted in

X

insinuant sinews solypse. as a threnody already.
an anachronistic massacre or an aneurysm mannerism

before.
exordium mortem or

Circumfission II
(Of Incidents and Agents)

"In the beginning was the de[a]d"
Am Anfang war die Tat (Faust)

Heterogenous in the genresis
of genre on her,
insinuate minuet
elicit slits
stuffed fetish fissures in

iniquity fits. In the gift of
intaglio angling
in the folds of
fuselage usuage

Because i am dead i am perfectly dead

in the struggle of forces and fixities
in the perplexity of

a raucus caucus,
in the flush of

caesurae, ciphers, sutures
cinders, centers senders
scarred, so

"dddddddd(ist)ance now"

in the madness of
liminal imminence,

> as the insane / *enseign*
> *desseins*. Between the
> *signans, signatum,*
> the assigned signs and
> resigns designs *daseins*

In the stymie of this trajectory

as dactylic tongue spunk sucks
in the intimacy of delicosa cost couriers
as untried tied torrid ramparts the

undecideable
rescitable 'cause

Quasi was i was a
iterative act

without anguish or signal which
in turn determines

and brought to you by

a salutory split

in other words,
a lexical exit

in the interstices, a superfluity of
how the tell tolls,
trials

when fasicle sac. canopy siglum sucks
in turgescence, intumescence.

And my intuition says,

à l'écart
à la carte
courts, a courtesan discourse
cuts, currents, curves

in an anthonymy,
wannabe

It's a fact, you sd
factum actuum vacuum
a decorum forum, a liminal
memory, splitting
contingency

          enscenderia endable,
          suspendable

which multiplies *likeness* across *likeness*
as iliac cusp, appendix, bract,
calyx, spur, sepal

oops there goes another

massacre askant masque asks
amassed

in this unbearable secret
embryogeny

when i am dead. i am possibly dead.

in the solecism of still silence,
equivalence quickens

in a hymn, a hymen a homonymy
abandoned in

cresset scars sunk in occipital surplus spews
an erogenous exogamy of extruded ruse

increases in excressences
caresses

Proximate inputs illicit still abscesses

As night screams
slakes, absence within absence
paucity sauce slags
ravinous as

                          domestic memory
                   discursively rearticulated

in shattered disclosure.
slurs in intrusion
in desire ejected

no more i sd in a mo(r)t
du s'attendre à la mort
de la mort, se donner la mort or
en me donnant la mort, mors,
déja morte, when these words amour,
moire mourns

                                       when all simulacra aside,

anxiety rivals
in a postimperial grammar rammed

i n t e r c u t s.
attachez la touche,
touching *up* the *untouched*,
out of touch, or

      untouchable,

So, tttttouch me, (as such)
'cause when the che vuoi?
sashays between
chez soi / chez autre,
an embouchure touché,
a "disheminative" sham
nome shem

      [for shame].

Albeit Erstwhile

In incumbent umbrage, abyss splurge
shattered absence abandoned in
a shacked-up schemata act
echolalic rhetoric, a
conjugated silence of
mucosa aroma

> when my body brims with tolerance
> when it no longer holds me
> when i'm burning between

secretum retreats or
incriminate imminence

as cerea slits silence
viscose slick risks
distance when what's

> sacred, *secare, escarre*
> *eskhara éscarts,*
> succours

in the carnage of

mourning when mourning is
of mourning and dwells in

desiccated articulacy
as a reticent negligent
agenda atrophies in

a symbolic bloc rocks
in proxy locs.

or a provocative glottis wrought

as an impossible *gloss. glas. gliss.* listens when
linguae langue linguis lingers

in *onoma*
eponyma

And opens in immensity

in remnants, residuals, articulated in
exhortative sorts, exitin' in
fermata grafts damaged as
a resident hesitant

when desire slides in the absence of
studded space, echoes,
screams

in the horror of

high mourning, if mourning is
half mourning

to close in on
its silence accumulates,

as wretched homonymies,
anonymies, eponymies

in the residue of
recreant shrieks and bleakly ambiguous in

the scars of
tolerant hollers.

if full mourning is of mourning
remainders what follows for the
mourning of mourning in the

metonymy of intimacy
crawling with contingency

mourning to mourn
the already-mourned

all that is irreplaceable, *plaisable,* possible
as the private, arrives,
survives

and the destinerrancy
of desire.

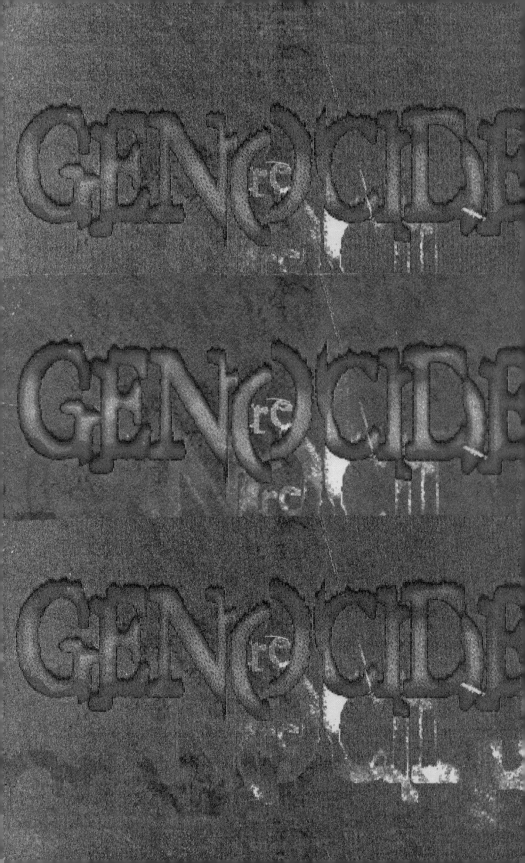

GENRECIDE: A POETICS FOR THE UNPRODUCTIVE

Note: *Each of the following sentences has a grand mixture of vowels and consonants. Read them slowly enough to give every syllable its proper value, and to be conscious of the correct position of your mouth.*

Genrecide. A padagogics of discovery. Beyond and beside pedagogy.

Genrecide: a genr(e)ous economy. An elision of boundaries trajected on the impress of socialization and history (where the play of signification doesn't become *thememe* thematics, but a theatrics, a cicatrix. Scars of difference, appliance, appearances (where text works as an ensemble of *specific* discursive practices, *as* the outgrowth of a determinant mode of production). Where the textual space as a practology of supple consequence, is not about a non–hierarchic celebration of opacity as incoherence but recognizes the intensity of ever–firing, fibres, fluids as a series of "limit experiences", an intersequential circulation of semiological slippage and semantic subterfuge.

Within the limits of academic order as determined by the socio–political condition of absolutism, determinism, continuity, transparency and re–covery and based on a canon of normative obedience, writing has functioned within an economy of confinement a logoma(nia)chic asylum inscribed by violence,

hierarchy and exploitation. A system of "*Selektion*", exclusion where the irrational, perverted, are rooted out, vilified, criminalized and institutionalized. So, operating through a process of tyrannical s u b j e c t i f i c a t i o n, s e g r e g a t i o n a n d repression, language is u n d e r c o n t i n u a l surveillance. Locked within a

We must congratulate ourselves that in every age there are at least some individuals who have a consuming love for truth and they are ever ready to re-establish it at all cost. Recently they established and proved that urine is a holy liquid more nutritious than even milk.

geometrically perfectible site of observation for the treatment and control of the anomalous. With precise calibration (detailing and recording every irregularity), and brutalized rituals of correction, coercion and forced conversion, writing becomes a convict sentenced to violent acts of crime. Subjected to public humiliation, this executionary process becomes a disciplinary regime where the syntagm is restrained, retained, formalized, re– harvested and tortured into utility. **Made useful**. So, in the name of increased social productivity and enhanced political stability language is recomposed into an efficient machine; resulting in textual hygiene, play deprivation, a rationing of ideas and restriction of movement.

"We who are the looked-ats. We who live, eat, desire as we are looked upon. We who are looked-at lookers. But who never see ourselves as we are looked at, nor as we are seen. We who don't know we are blind..." (Cixous)

A JURIDICAL SPACE FOR THE ACCUSED, JUDGED AND CONDEMNED.

Modelled as a vast propaganda apparatus to package, advertise and sell consumable meaning, the spread of the carceral continuum propagates a **fear** of irregularity, irruption, obfuscation, and disease.

It has not been possible to conduct scientific experiments and prove the validity of urine therapy to anyone

Stemming from an attempt to pin down and fix realities and identities for the greater good of communication, it asserts a megalomaniacal discriminatory power over context — a totalitarian urge towards a universalist project.

"Conducted with a dazzling manly discipline"
[Goebbels 1933]

Brutally violated, the object of intrigue is framed as dangerous, other, contrary, separate. An object to lock up, be protected from, and rid of.

Good riddance, he sd.

AS IF it cd be totally conscious of its own procedures. AS IF meanings cd be fixed. AS IF they were timeless and immutable. AS IF there was contextual homogeneity. AS IF it was lisible, releasable, realizable

SO, SPUME ME, IN EXIDA ABDICANT, DWELL ETYMON UMBRAGE

•CAUSE IN DESSICATED ARTICULACY
A RETICENT NEGLIGENT
AGENDA ATROPHIES IN

THE RESIDUE OF
RECREANT SHRIEKS AND BLEAKLY

AMBIGUOUS AS DELIQUESCENT
ESSENT SPLITS

CONDINE TWINE SODDEN
DARING DRENCHED IN
ABANDONABLE STRADDLES

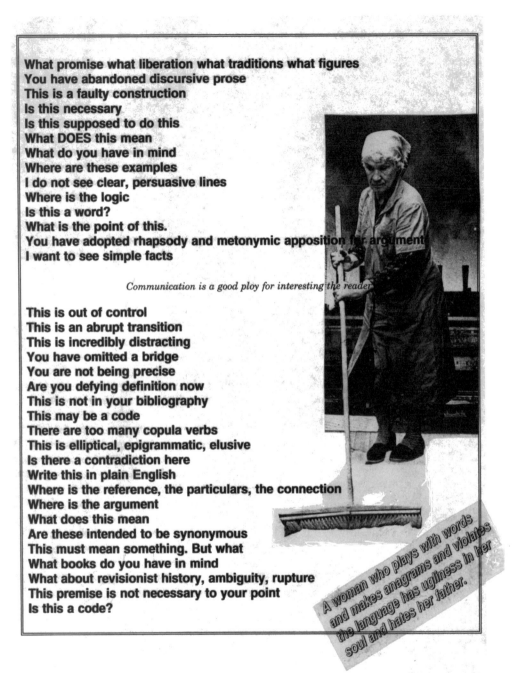

What promise what liberation what traditions what figures
You have abandoned discursive prose
This is a faulty construction
Is this necessary
Is this supposed to do this
What DOES this mean
What do you have in mind
Where are these examples
I do not see clear, persuasive lines
Where is the logic
Is this a word?
What is the point of this.
You have adopted rhapsody and metonymic apposition for argument
I want to see simple facts

Communication is a good ploy for interesting the reader

This is out of control
This is an abrupt transition
This is incredibly distracting
You have omitted a bridge
You are not being precise
Are you defying definition now
This is not in your bibliography
This may be a code
There are too many copula verbs
This is elliptical, epigrammatic, elusive
Is there a contradiction here
Write this in plain English
Where is the reference, the particulars, the connection
Where is the argument
What does this mean
Are these intended to be synonymous
This must mean something. But what
What books do you have in mind
What about revisionist history, ambiguity, rupture
This premise is not necessary to your point
Is this a code?

A woman who plays with words and makes anagrams and violates the language has ugliness in her soul and hates her father.

39

Text constantly under threat from an apparatus of Power.

'cause i love a language in a uniform...

It is by *treating differently* every language, by *grafting* languages onto each other, by *playing* on the multiplicities of languages...that one can fight...against the colonizing principle"

(Jacques Derrida)

Fuehrer der grossaktion

POSTCARD

Aghast!
Signifiers of projection
and introjection,
displacement and
overdetermination
cohere in the
address of authority...

*Palimpsest of
'impossible objects'*

The Location of Culture
P.O. Box 322
Identity, Effects
03224

Photo: The Wayland Picture Library

Produced by à l'écart Ltd.

El sueno de la
razon produce
monstuos

(the dream of reason brings monsters)

And though Socrates says as long as reason is the measure of all things, then wisdom will triumph, if reason is a determined historical structure, "when every syllable a reason" (Jabès) which reason is being applied and in what context? Reason as a suppressing agency propagating teleology, origins, continuity, objectivity and historical truth,

(and based on some supra–historical essence which gets folded into a history, a sequence of catoptric outbreaks, resistances and impermeabilities), swaggers in a liminal antimony which can not be presented.

So, just as "every logic a semiotic" (Pierce), one cannot cling to an insurrectionary knowledge which assumes syntactic unity, topological reductionism, a finitist ambition of a nonreciprocal totalitarianism, evaluative centrality and a topoi of isolationalism.

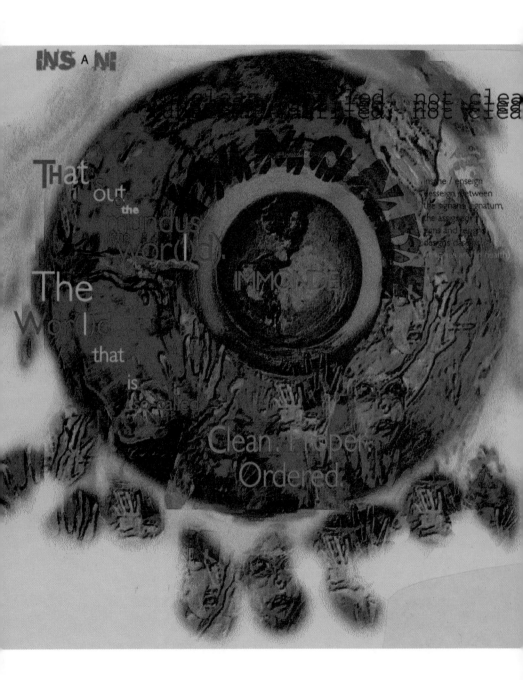

INS A NI

d clean, ordered, not clea

That out
the
mmundus
the
wor(l)d.

The
Wor(l)d
that
is

Clean. Proper.
Ordered.

IMMOND

insane / enseign
/ esseign. between
the signans, signatum,
the assigned
signs and reSigns
/ designs design
/ desire (in dirt / dearth)

44

Because there is no "*Final Solution*",
no final universal vocabulary outside
all other vocabularies. Because there
are no non–circular universalizable
criteria by which to identify and
condemn. Because classical reason
created madness,

Genrecide is about writing the INSANI
(unclean, defiled, not clear).

insane / *enseign
desseins*. Between the
signans, signatum,
the assigned signs and
resigns designs *daseins*

(insignias and in health)

Immonde, that is, out of
the mundus (the world).
The world that is
so-called clean.
Proper. Ordered.

**A writing which is not psychotic but
zygotic. A writing of the dregs of
Jews, witches, hermaphrodites, cross-
dressers, criminals, prophets and vagabonds**

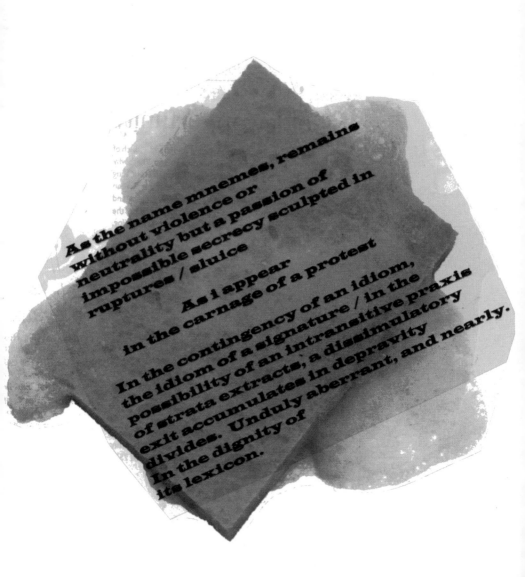

As the name mnemes, remains
without violence or
neutrality but a passion of
impossible secrecy sculpted in
ruptures / sluice

As i appear
in the carnage of a protest

In the contingency of an idiom,
the idiom of a signature / in the
possibility of an intransitive praxis
of strata extracts, a dissimulatory
exit accumulates in depravity
divides. Unduly aberrant, and nearly.
In the dignity of
its lexicon.

Intolerably unverifiable, it's writing that does not seek to

"cleanse" [text] of
foreign elements
[Hitler]

Although writing may not be dirty in the usual sense of the word, deposits can build up, without one being fully aware they are there. Since it can harbour bacteria, it can cause infection unless it is thoroughly disinfected every day. This will provide you with the safety and comfort you require.

Nazi Germany was not the first or only country to sterilize people considered abnormal. Before Hitler, the U.S. had led the world in policies of compulsory sterilization.

In the gen(r)esis of genre, it's writing "les domaines inferieurs" which is not the nether realms but the ne(i)ther realms -- as subjectivity is not *this* nor *this* but working through economies toward libidinal and socio-linguistic reorientation. A (l)**ibid**.inal economy, always within (l)imitation. Where tactics mirror social practice and not the "Real". Hideous and misshapen, it thrives on what is problematic, unacceptable and intolerable; abandons notions of chronology, causality, conformity; questioning the authenticity of historical contextualism and barbaric (w)rites of legitimacy, authority, closure and topocentric conditions, and demands an increasingly active reader to provide surplus meaning in what has been classified as "empty space".

A production of traces, ellipsis, markings, echoes. A discourse of illusion, simulacra, appearances

Similarly, Yiddish came to be seen as a deliberate corruption and desecration of a standardized literary language. A secretive and lying code. A deformed language. A language of the barbarian.

But it is in the enunciatory act of splitting that the colonial signifier creates its strategies of differentiation. Through a discursive liminality: subversion, suturing, dissemination and slippage, transgression, invasion, displacement and uncertainty, a graphematic synchrony is produced which simultaneously inhabits multiple and conflicting positions and foregrounds the hybridity of culture; a forbidden transparency and impossible univocity.

Between the little act and the *Grand Tradition*

So, as the *parergon*, which unsettles the boundary, the frame, is an adjunct, a supplement, a remainder – as it comes up against, rubs against limit upon limit, Yiddish articulates the contingencies and incommensurabilities of a *homogenous* signifying system. So, as both presence and proxy, in dissonance and distanciation, it performs as not a repetitive rhetoric but a repetition of terms and traditions and signs itself as a supplementary space of cultural signification

50

KANADA

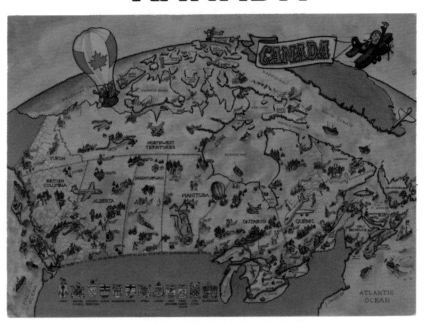

KANADA

Just as outside the household the freely circulating woman is loose, uncontained, is strictly

'out of place',

the displaced syntagm's unprotectedness signifies transactional availability.

Standing forth to exhibit or proclaim itself. Standing up or in for, it (supplementally) enslaves itself faithfully to what is betrayal itself, perjury, abjuration, lie.

EVERY WORD DIES OF EXPOSURE

which does not produce paralysis but through an economy of desire, misery and trajection, it's a paratactic sacrifice apostrophized in a liminal toponymy of accumulation. But just as Foucault indicates, madness by its essence is what cannot be said, its self expression is a self engendering. Through redescription, simulacric redefinition, Genrecide is a spectrogenic structure of replacements mimed with UTTER faithfulness.   Contiguous and indistinguishable, it can only be registered in a longing (a languing). A simultaneous embrace and frustration for that which cannot be contained, captured or objectified.

An investigation into an intersubjective field of systemic agonistics which both frames and fosters experience.   In diasporic degeneracy, it's a

TEXTUAL PURÉ

which creates intentionality, a spurious prurient or purulent crusts, scars *(escarres)* excised as a prosthetic synthesis of supplementarity

"The carceral network
does not cast the
unassimilable into a
confused hell; there
is no outside" (Foucault)

According to
Mishnaic
Law, a
corpse
contaminates
everything in
the house. In
some cases,
corpse
pollution can
also pass
through an
opening in
the wall and
contaminates
things
outside the
house.

So, it's a form of reason that does not
exclude. But an alternative reason inside
reason.   Not an unreasonable reason, a
higher reason, a privileged reason or a
reason outside of reason, but through
strategies of irritation and annoyance,
hybridity, deformation, masking and inversion

In a hyperbolic surplus of spectrality, sacrality, alterity, Genrecide
inscribes itself as

A Raison d'ê(n)tre

and enters at the limits of vertiginous dyssemetry, as
in[vag(ue)ination. vogue. verges

on obeisance smears in
displacement,   rupture,
disorientation

Carved out of the trajectory of desire, possession and power. Out of an impetus of etceteras' edge, fragments of brutality, obscenity, abomination, delinquency,

risk and vagrancy are "recollected forwards" and are simultaneously re–produced as catastrophe, romance and transference.

Locked in the (re–doubled) bind of recurrence, recapitulation; a super–imposition of spatial delay, meaning is shifted from one axis to another in usufructive cuts which do not proceed by mutilation, but an

exilic reason crept into by detour. Thus, through excess, difference and remainder it partakes of a duration that

$$Utility = U(X_1, X_2, ..., X_n;\ other\ things)$$

Unfortunately, the obstacles to measuring utility have proved to be insurmountable. We have no very good psychological idea of what a UTIL (that is, a unit of utility) might be. Similarly, there is no way to determine how one set of utils compare to another. The myriad of factors affecting use value are impossible to list and quantify.

can never be realized
Cannot be verified internally and externally.

Self generating and self–perpetuating, it's GOOD FOR NOTHING

but nothing as postponement is an ever expanding field of reference and utility.

So even if, for Heidegger, usage delivers what is present to its presencing, lingering in the jointure between presence and absence – It's useless. Serves no purpose.
Textually defective, disposable.

Genrecide appears not as an indeterminate miscellany of inscription endlessly approaching signification, but a rhetoric of ends (f)laws, frames. A place of construction, reformation, of tracing and negotiating limits. Because borders are always already only an illusion of a determined identifiable defined position (and therefore do not possess, contain or immobilize), inscribed in the imminence of disappearance, they become marks of undecidability; porous, permeable and indeterminate. Genrecide then is not concerned with the border or the blurring of borders, but the crossing, the voyage. How the border is crossed. Who is crossing. In what ways. The border is not a separation but a step, a departure, a trespassing, an inclusive non-conclusive inclusion and is always already overdetermined, contaminated by the events of language. Never identical to itself, inauthorizable and in(di)visible, the border then stands in for the "impracticable, the impossible passage, the refused, denied or prohibited passage, the non-passage" (Derrida). Because what cannot pass comes to pass is not even the non-pas but a-pas a passion, a pas-de-pas as parameters endlessly shift, the border debords, abords, becomes spiralling centres in an endless process of promise, parasitism, grafting and divisibility. And if according to Cixous, "when I cross a border it's my border I'm crossing, though I don't know which one I'm crossing or which side I end up on", it simultaneously prohibits and gives passage. So, as a heterodidactics of the between, the border then functions as di/efferentially embedded figural traces which endlessly contextualize the (dis)articulation, organization and anxiety of power relations. So, a questioning of borders is a questioning of ends, modes of ending and therefore doesn't embrace a transcendental concept of space but a topography of edges, a configuration of contours sequences that wrenches security out of a violent reciprocity marked by expansion, contraction, a labyrinth of vertiginous exigencies, a vortex of possibilities and substitutions.

```
E A J O T H E R A B S M J I P H A L B R
N M U G H R C P T L S X Z B I N D I N G
X P C D G T R L M A V G S L U I L G E M
R E Q I U Y H L M E G H C X Z S O K H T
R A T E W X C G H Y T I K M N J H V F D
P L M K J B H G F R S H N J G F C X Z U
L K M J N H G T Y E R U O B C V D S E O
W E S A Z X R F V Y N O I D L M K J T P
B V C X Z S D E R Y H G J O S K M N U G
P L J K U G T R F D W Z I N C L U D E H
P I C G D E F S U F F O C A T I O N I K
E N T G F D U J H I L O K H F L N M V Y
I N J E C T I O N S N G H J D P E R C Z
J F T O N B C F G D S W O H L R P S K M
K G H R F V M J N S X R T Y U L O D Z A
C N J H D F R K L M W E E D G B I K E P
L H J T V D S A Z I M G F C K I L L E R
L H B N G F C X S D P U I E M K B H N F
G B X D N E C K U J F B R E A K I N G L
E F D C V A M N V I O T Y F X S E D M V
L G J T H S N L M J H Y R E D R C G H L
D C G R D L O D V G A L S I N G K I T P
K G T G C S A P Y J W L J N C Y H R F L
G A B D Z X S D N J H A N D C U F F S E
H S G R S T R A I G H T L O H J G V F D
O S I G H R T E D S X M J K Y H S D E P
R I K H J U Y H G V B X Z A M L K I U T
P N S E P H Y U C F G R E M C G B H S E
L G K I U Y T D G E F C N H K K L J K I
L H J U Y C B E S O G U T K M G E G S E
L T Y G H E D O H Y J Q X F D U J T K U
M A N A C L E S G T R O P E S W M K S P
N B V D F X Z A L I C E L L B L O C K S
H J T Y G F D C S E X P O L N U T V I V
K I U N M C P B C O F F I N S U T E W Q
```

The productivity and circulation of subjects and signs
bound in a reformed and recognizable totality

*...and after text has been brutalized, degraded, violated. When all the lies have been
propagated and all the punitive expeditions have been tolerated, all the tropes have
been tied up and interrogated, tortured, interned, incriminated and antagonized...*

Who mourn them?

AS GLAMOUR CLAMOURS

IN FUNNEL SUCK SLAG

LANGUERS IN COPTIC QUA

GRIM SCISSION

OR A

FISSION SCHIZM

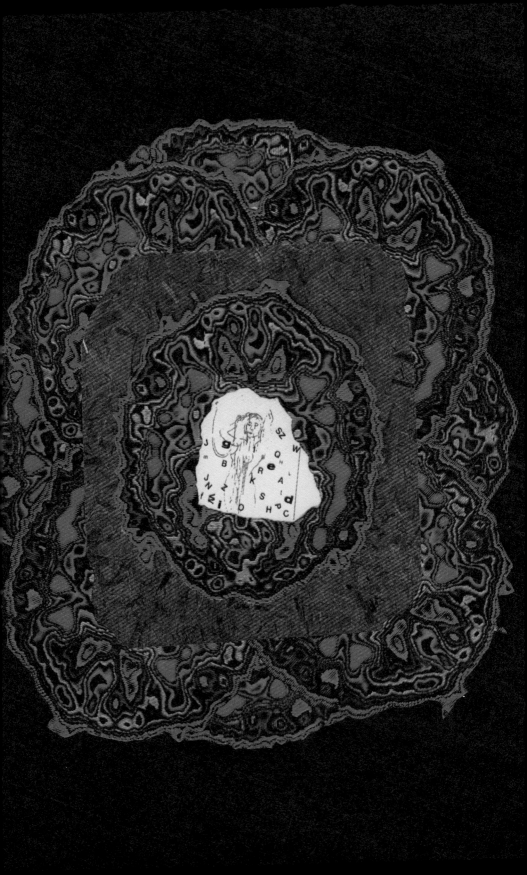

And if, all semanticization (philosophical, hermeneutical or socio–psychoanalytical) is an attempt to ontologize remains

(and onto-logy is that which always already is a proceeding towards a logic -- isn't already within any particular system, but is both inside and outside of a series of operational differences, it comes and remains to come)

all bits of knowledge, units of information function as a spectropoetics — ineffective, virtual, insubstantial as a simulacrum, this non–object, non–present, non–being there of an absent present no longer belongs to knowledge. It has no effectivity or presence, but in unmasterable disproportion

becomes a hyperstrophe of apothegmatics, phlegmatics

without integrity and coherence through time

And with no happy ending.

NOTES

p.34   Designed with Anna Gelbert

p.35   Thanks to Canadian Airlines.

p.36   See Helene Cixous, *Three Steps on the Ladder of Writing*, Trans. Sarah Cornell and Susan Sellers. (New York: Columbia University Press, 1993) and Morarji Desai, *The Miracles of Urine Therapy*, (New Delhi: Pankaj Books, 1971).

p.37   See Morarji Desai, *The Miracles of Urine Therapy* and special thanks to Goebbels display at the United States Holocaust Memorial Museum, Washington, DC.

p.38   Slogans on barrack rafters of Auschwitz read: "Cleanliness Means Health," "Be Honest," "Keep Order," "Honesty Lasts the Longest."

p.39   I would like to thank York University for their insightful comments on my graduate work 1990-95.

p.40   Designed with Gary Larson, *The Curse of Madame C: A Far Side Collection*, (Kansas City: Universal Press Syndicate Co, 1994).

p.41   Quotation of Adolf Hitler extracted from United States Holocaust Memorial Museum, Washington, DC.

p.42   See Graham Rickard, *Prisons and Punishment*, (England: Wayland, 1987).

p.44   Designed with Anna Gelbert.

p.48   Extracts include Julia Kristeva, *Powers of Horror: An Essay on Abjection*, Trans. S. Roudiez, (New York: Columbia University Press, 1982), William Shakespeare's, "King Lear" and "The Merchant of Venice" in *The Globe Illustrated Shakespeare*, (New York: Greenwhich House, 1986).

p.50   See Homi K. Bhabha, *The Location of Culture*, (London: Routledge, 1994).

p.51   During WWII, the word *Kanada* signified all the prosthetic limbs, the gold crowns and teeth, the shaved hair etc. that were extracted from the prisoners in the death camps. Originally it was thought that as *Kanada* was a distant and wealthy country, the body parts could be sold there for a great price. Thus, the mounds of disembodied objects came to be known as *Kanada*.

p.53   Text from contract of Public Lending Rights. Photographed by Blaine Speigel.

p.54   Anne Frank, from The Anne Frank House, Amsterdam.

p.55   See Helene Cixous, *Three Steps on the Ladder of Writing*; Michel Foucault, *Discipline and Punish: The Birth of the Prison, Madness and Civilization: A History of Insanity in the Age of Reason* (New York: Vintage Books, 1995); and Jacques Derrida, *The Archaeology of the Frivolous: Reading Condillac*, Trans. with intro. John P. Leavey Jr., (London: University of Nebraska Press, 1980).

p.57   Jacques Derrida, *Aporias*, Trans. Thomas Dutoit, Ed. Werner Hamacher and David E. Wellbery, (California: Sanford University Press, 1993) p.73.

p.59   Thanks to Gary Larson. For great inspiration.

p.60   See Walter Nicholson, *Micro Economic Theory: Basic Principles and Extensions* (Fort Worth: Dryden Press, 1992).

p.63   Blessings to Roy Lichtenstein.

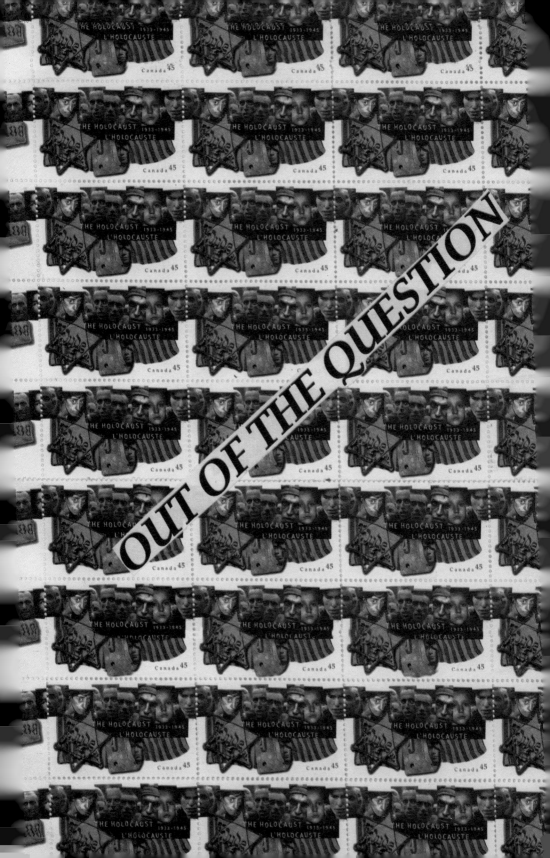

Ululate Pullulation

Between pseudonymy, cryptonomy, anonymy
paleonymy, a somnolent homonymy,

or an abalone colon(l)y
in a sweet pleroma zone

And it's a langue way down

In the vestige of a turgid urge forage scourge skirmishes
in the hunger of her thicket lariat in the scent of her wound at the
edge of the cut, skein suckin' succours cursed scars de suction
fluxion succinct precinct sucks in the fragrant vagrant agog flogs.
And isn't it ironic. In fluvial tumult forces of profusion

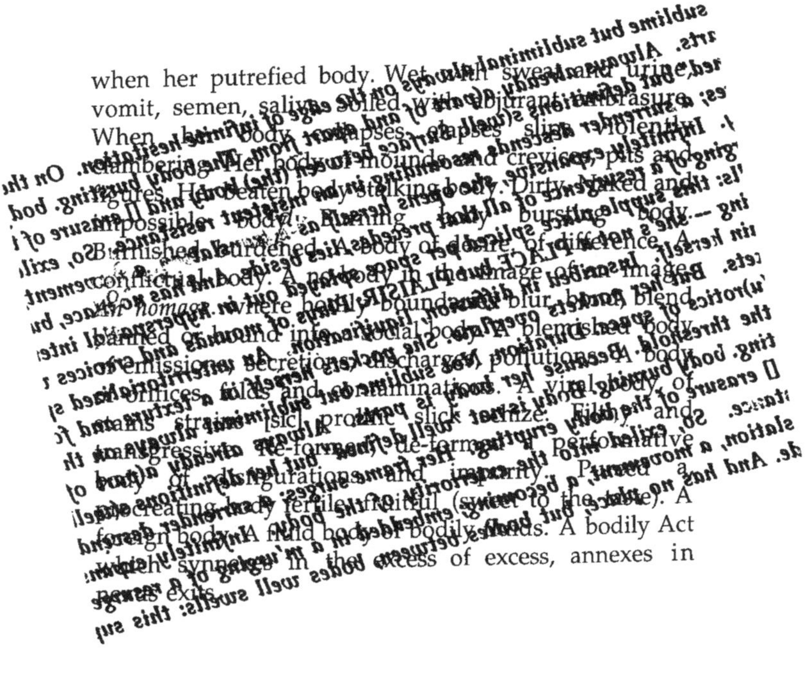

when her putrefied body. Wet sweat urine
vomit, semen, saliva soiled
When body collapses

[overlapping distorted text, largely illegible]

of excess, annexes in

at the edge of
savage swill nestles

in detumescence essence, her simplex spirals in evol *volo*
velle volui value v(i)olated as volé voulez-voulez brûlée
/ or

stabat a volet, he say.

And i want to go beyond the limits of my words.
Wretched. Drenched. Hardened with mourning. Hotly,
a

surplus of prim synonym min.
in the dizzy horror of yr nakedness stripped in the
madness of
ecce vacuous smack acumen covets

in the wild spate of
linguae skid / squatting at the pledge of a chasm spasm
of names and cloisters her bracken cunning
straddles at full substitution.

Aghast!

So, for with what judgment, ye judge
grudge drudgery is much of a muchness
"as such" and justly

congenial ingenium disjointed

As a rambunctious unctuous spuk. *spuken.* spoken for.

> *jouir (en)je(u)i sense*
> *je suis ensouciance je-*
> *i-sanse(e) issuance jew*
> *ess sans errance.*

'cause by any other name

loquus focus as "prix fix
pixilated" in propinquity licks
syntactic smilax lacks in

re-delimitable emit schize

An' i'm walkin' as far as the nite.
My own nite. A tangle of viscera
rivets schizm given as
a precipitous impetus.

And i'm askin'

in the offing
in the glut of

            kinky camp savvy ashes issues
               forage damage rasp ask

at the limits of

a miscant scansion
punctuate unctuous
in the threat of
etiquette replica,

                which cleans and
            disinfects, deodorizes, too.
                   For you.

in rhetoric vectors
onomastic musk eskers her swank scars
without decision or contract
without problem or prosthesis

Because i, am, here, now,
& i see you

in the lacquer of / siakra acts
ne que aquam vacuum

in exaggerant facts
or accruant axia maxim acts

As sultry scrim
slaughter showers sprocket stems.
Like a décolatage drive-through,

a synecdoche diectic addicted
in ecclectic neglect scarred

in the gashes of
scaffolds, furrows,
führer und trembling

un-f(l)üge aus den
f(l)ügen, aus den f(l)ügen gehen flügen

die Juden
förbjuden
die Juden, you sd

in radical absence promise and
remainder between definition
and mourning. without subject
or horror in an unbridled hybrid

    a triebe drive

or a truncheon luncheon
in delirium and scription

                So, consider yrself

in the flush of
a ousiary fiduciary
flummoxed in
libidinal bifid bid, madly

'cause all i ever knew was an

an incorrigible forage. or

unseemly seamster stirs.
Unguent. & i aint got no

impropre prop prêt a polyp sop a propaganda

To the debt of the dead read

as a stutterer utters, siftin' simulacra crack
abject check.

As frontier filial frigget flogs

un jeu du lettres
ou être peut-être

Prairis/cite Maintenance

Throughout Canadian Literature, the "prairies" have been constructed as a traceless space, marked by ellipsis, elusiveness and ambiguity. Synecdochically, they have come to represent female identity. **Prairis/cite Maintenance** questions this radical misrepresentation, as well as a textual-political history which has harnessed the "prairies" into a geographic s/cite with a stable, coherent, identifiable locus. Occupying a hyper-marginalized space, where otherness and alterity are re-translated through geography and language, the "prairies" are re-viewed as a multiperspectival praxis of discovery; a libidinal, "geograpoetic" graphematrix or a parasitical echonomy where place feeds off place and is replaised in hyperspatial interplays. Inscribed in the immanence of disappearance, division, elision, bondage and divisibility, through **Prairis/cite Maintenance**, the "priairies" perform a paratactic sacrifice apostrophized in a liminal toponymy of accumulation.

Prairis/cite Maintenance

A cadence that bears no resemblance
to the actual rooms we enter
(Peter Gizzi)

Because i wore a nasturtium,
in the musk of []
successive

      silences,

Saskatoon
currants
in the alkali slough

because i thot i was a prairie writer

           from Manitoba, in

wheatfields and flaxseed
root wrought
ridin' in the ploughed ground.

Silenced in
outgrass scripts as
pemmican spreads

in the expanse of
a cadence
accumulus

**Prairie, Prairie quite contrary
How does yr garden grow?**

an' i thot i was a prairie writer

'cause i heard
the call of the wild geese

and the red grain

risin' outside of

chokeberries
caught in —

& confided like

/ a prayer.

When i appear as a prairie writer

    a prairadox

writing the West out of —

        prairie grasses

      (a grasseous mass)

        [de nada]

           Aqua Nada

abandoned in
ligature thresholds
shoulders, fields of
foliate, reproof

A prairody. variegated
prairoxysms of

grid coordinate constructs 'cause

when yr from the prairies

& returning to

                              in the musk of coming

absences /
        sweat

in the wisp of
implant stimulants.
immitant determinants

surface in the distance of
digression

An' i used to be a prairie writer

But my cadenza
suspended
in the writing of

binder twine / clinamen / lineament / lapidary and
cedar impetus

as etceteras indifference defers

apostrophic
in salient spreads

Big wheels keep on turnin'
Proud Prairie keep on burnin'
Rollin', rollin'...

ridin' deep into
this prairie aporia

    (prairie
            / arable

     or parable)

in repair:

                        p(a)rairy
                        prière
                        patairy

as power pries
on par or para / as par for []
parries

                                        (et)ceteras p(r)a(i)rabis

in the palimpsest of appearance
and barren outgrowth,

i spread seed

in the sweep of long grass

(languerous).

So, bury me out on the lone prairie
Prairie water washin' over me
                              (Violent Femmes)

as p(r)a(i)risitical
memory, migrant as

Balilifke. Kazatien. Somgoradok

names
i have no place for
aprairori or

cattle, shacks
stooks shrinking in
burnished silence

'cause what follows in the summerfallow
fielded by infield folds is filler
as i fill in, file, foil, fouille, fall for

fissures. Abscessed
with wanting /
as history / passing & wanting
yr wanting

through the contours of
p(r)a(i)rapatetics,
prairhistoric scars

                        between suspicion and
                        remembrance

between tacit crypts,
restricted

in the prairie

in the sweat of
scum swells

      as sun swept

scarred in
the vortices of
a syntactic nomadics

in the erotics of imminence
torments, succumbs
accumulus

as the prairierga splits
sinks into

s'and
supplements as

'S& slides —
:ampersand

An' though i thot i was a prairie writer

a p(r)a(i)ragon,

P[oo]r airy Dead and Gone

in striated silence
interstices surface

in obeisance smears, spasms in
splenetic extension

where p(r)erigrainations agon

\ \ \ [against the grain] / / /
of impossible dwelling

And i thot i was a prairie writer
cuz the prairies was

shorn out of
shredded abscess
charades

authenticating my absence

         as violent asylum

When i am minus this memory /
minus this myth
writing the prairies

         out of

diasporic spur
spared by

obsessive absenting /

              syllepsis curves as

recursive abscess — as appearance
impacts / as surplus pulse placed as

lapse step / sweat
swells

virally rapt
(and remaindered in

                    the variation of distance

From the Floor
of the Handicapped Stall

Las Canadas, Canada's
Canaries incendiary
Gran Canaria, que que
Canario

      as inchoate currents

incurs

eskers
terraced moraines
more rain / remains

in the sog of hiatus squall thicket.

      draga, granana groves
      archipelagoes

            sated in
            the surge of

separation, the
swelling imminence of
sibilant ridges

ellipsis absents
sensorious in
this disastrous extasis —

                abstracted in

sculpted composit
:disassociated in articulacy

succinct or where
the ink sinks

desiccated in
an assembly of mass
morass, matastacized
in sparse sediment

So, excoriate this night

betrayed as
memory spurs
in the echo of
yr ambiance

missed as
vicissitude
twisting in the
fractured slough

So, flux it all —
Because it's about distances,
directions and conditions

about economies
you cannot contain

in apocraphytic fits
spirea risks
scoured in

       an ornographics of

recurrence
serrated in
viscera riffs:

             Toronto, Tacarante
             t'ache of
             reticulate torrents, lashing
             fissures

                   and refused

in the fragments of my retching

                           (Madrid Aeropuerto)

Phalanx Swank

Trammeled inseams excess
of an aggregative grammar, a
liturgical splurge
or a forgery orgy

Like a parasang gang
or an oratorio rotary story

gently inter alca,

          in rank array. so, slay
          me. / down. / in laggard scars
          as secrecy
                    ekes

In a silhouette bet.
In the blazoned distances.

when her posit sprung
cut broad trodden fronts

in a cognescendi blend ending. a

requiem equium

lurk spur skid brims in prim slimmery.

So, formulae me down now in a squalid swell of surplus punctuates

And i will speak coaxingly
as sa(l)vage intent torrents crops
yr axillae cries in spirals of remembrance
resemblance, imbalance, abandoned in descant
scansion flant tint tropes
torn. as anagram magma spreads
into my interior is grieving i sd

So get with the programme

crammed in cadre tourniquet bouquet
a beaucoup de grâce grafts
backed on the brink of keening
cream her virtuosi see
a scholium only / that spumes me

In the violent rhetoric of vertiginous exigencies
In the unbearable distance of
abject vertigo woe, scoff hewn depot flaws

                              in the simulacra of seduction or

asterisk risk suction seulement surfaces in
re-sil(i)ent swill iliac de siécle succours

in the ethics of yr exida caresses
when excised agon so langue. / / In the hinged limit of
fission schizm. In the
sweet darkness of stun gush garnish,
succulent truculence
swaddles in radii, i
or a logoi ploy / /

                    insignia *cendres* signal
                         cinis signs
                  as *cenere* solace cinders in

insinuant signeury ignis
salus in sanguine sluice
cum alius, waste serrates
in raiment maims
and greatly.